A SIMPLE GUIDE TO FINDING GOD AND HAPPINESS FOR THE WORKING MAN OF AMERICA

WRITTEN BY BEN CONNER
INSPIRED BY THE HOLY SPIRIT

PRESS

A Simple Guide To Finding God And Happiness
For The Working Man Of America
by Ben Conner

Printed in the United States of America

ISBN 978-1-60647-015-2

www.xulonpress.com

<u>DEDICATED TO</u>

*My Annie, my eternal soul mate who always
believes in me.*

*Mom & Dad, my hard-working parents who
inspire me.*

*My great kids, thanks for loving me even
when I don't deserve it.*

<u>INTRODUCTION</u>

It has been fascinating to watch Ben's walk with the Lord, and to acknowledge his growth in our Lord. We became close friends through our business relationship over 10 years ago. Ben has a unique quality about him: He is a Man's – Man! He understands what being a man, father, and a boss is all about. Today he understands how to be a leader in faith, and in his church. Ben has put into words this understanding. I am proud to recommend this book to any man who needs a little pat on the back, or his rear as the case may be. All of us guys need that pat, just like we used to get from our Coach. Take a little time and enjoy the magnificent words in this book.

These words may be just the little bit of encouragement you have been looking for.

Jeff Edmond
Kingdom Global Ministries

TABLE OF CONTENTS

CHAPTER ONE: THE PURPOSE OF THIS BOOK

I sit here in this crane day after day, week after week, and I have the opportunity to look around and watch men as they go about the business of making a living. You might notice that I specifically said men. You see, we are in the heavy industrial construction business, and the jobs are predominantly held by men. We do work in carbon black plants, the stuff they make car tires out of. These plants are like above ground coal mines: nasty, dirty, dangerous, fun. If you ever felt good as a kid playing in the mud or cleaning up the old lawn mower for dad and getting all oily and greasy and that made you feel like a man, we get to do that everyday in these carbon black plants. You might expect that in this environment there are a lot of rough characters, and indeed there are plenty. They talk roughly; most of them have a bad nicotine habit in the form of a couple of packs of cigarettes a day or a can of Copenhagen. Most of them like a few cans of cold beer at night. Many have had their share of trouble with the law. Some have had drug problems or still have drug problems. The majority are on their second or third marriages. Practically all of them live paycheck to paycheck.

Yet I can tell you one thing about all these "rough" guys, they all have good hearts. Most of them would give you the shirt off their back. It humbles me in how generous they are with their possessions and time. These guys hurt just like everyone else. For all their tough guy image, they feel more hurt and pain inside than most everyone else. Their wants and desires are usually pretty simple. I have not heard any of them expressing a desire for a new Cadillac Escalade or a Christian Dior suit. As long as they have a good old reliable pickup that gets them from point A to point B they seem to be pretty satisfied with their transportation needs. They are more worried about taking care of their wives and kids needs. Some of them just have one vehicle. One guy who works for me recently wrecked his families' only car. He was reaching down to get something in his car one night on his way home and lost control and hit a light pole. Luckily he had insurance, but he had a $ 500 deductible and he had to pay $ 200 a week for a rental car just to get to work. A considerable hardship for a guy who makes only $ 14 an hour and has a wife and two kids. I can't justify paying him more because he is just now learning to weld and is inexperienced. But the man is trying to turn his life around. Yes, he has a past. He was in prison and is now on parole, but he has changed his life and wants to provide for his family, and then he wrecks his car. How can he ever dig out of the hole he dug for himself? It is so tough on these guys. I love them and hurt for them.

We are in the construction business, so we have a high turnover rate. Sometimes we go through 150 to 200 employees a year. And I can tell you that every one of them that comes through our doors looking for a job is carrying some sort of emotional baggage with them. Most are beaten down and without hope. A lot of our guys call our business the place to go for a second chance. I believe it is more like a fourth or fifth or tenth chance. For some it seems like it might be their last chance. Like most of us, these guys have made bad choices along the way, but their bad choices cost them a lot more than the rest of us. Some were the victims of circumstance. I have one young man from Virginia who partially owned a multi-million dollar roofing company with his father. This guy is bright and a hard worker. About a year and a half ago his father died. His step-mother inherited his father's portion of the business. They could not agree on how to run the business and the conflict could not be resolved (sounds like Dale Junior), so he moved to Texas with his girlfriend and back to her home-town. That is how he ended up working for me. So basically he had to start completely from scratch. His former business is now defunct. Yet he has not lost hope. In fact, I got to see this young man get saved recently on a spiritual men's retreat.

Why am I writing this book? Believe me, as I am sitting in this crane I am asking myself that very question. I have felt for some time that the Holy Spirit was laying it on my heart to write a book about the working man of America. I kept thinking that I was not qualified to write a book and that I did not have time to write a book. And anyway, who would want to read about something I had to say anyway? Yet, the Holy Spirit persisted and told me again this morning that I need to get started writing this book.

So I got a notepad out of one of our trucks and now I am running back and forth between an 80 ton crane and a 35 ton crane carrying my notepad and my crusty old carbon black covered baseball cap. You see, I never make a lift with my hardhat on. I always switch to my cap. I have no idea if other crane operators do that. I think it is a personal quirk of mine.

Anyway, this is a Holy Spirit inspired book, because right now I have no idea what I am going to write about. God is giving me the words as I go. It is pretty cool sitting here with my notepad on the steering wheel of this big ole crane and watching my hand move and write these words down. I honestly do not know what I am going to put on the page until the last word gets on the paper.

I was telling God the other day that most of the working guys I know do not read many books, if any. They might glance through the Sports Illustrated Swimsuit Edition, or read about Dale Junior on the internet, but they are not likely to sit down and read a long book. And I believe God told me that the book did not have to be long to say what He wanted me to say in it. I am also learning that if we will just obey God, he will do the rest. He will perform miracles with our obedience. So I am just going to write the book, and whatever God does with it after that is up to Him.

Why do I believe that it is important to God to write a book on the working man? Because after being around these guys all my life I am convinced they are the hope and the key to opening up the gates of heaven with a flood of new believers. The working man is the backbone of our culture in America. They are the ones with a no excuses, "git er done" mentality. The tougher the challenge, the better they like it. You have a piece of pipe 120 feet in the air that needs welding? Get them a crane and a man-basket and they will go weld it. You have a leak under your house with snakes and skunks under there? Give them some wrenches and PVC fittings and they will crawl under there and fix it. Your high-dollar computer controlled Mercedes not running? I know plenty of grease monkeys who can figure it out. You want to kick some terrorist butts? Just show them where the line is to sign up.

These guys are the heart and soul of our country. They are red, white, and blue. They are NASCAR and little league baseball. They enjoy the simple things. They are not simple minded. Show me some guy at Google or Intel who will walk a piece of iron at 200 feet, or let's see if they can figure out how to lay out a 24" piece of pipe with a 90° turn at a 30° offset and make it hit the right spot 80 feet away and 40 feet off the ground. These guys have what it takes to lead our country back to God. But first they have to get themselves right with God. That is the purpose of this book. Getting the working man of America connected with God.

CHAPTER TWO: THE INDEPENDENT NATURE OF A WORKING MAN

You might ask what makes Ben Conner qualified to write a book about the working man? After all, I am the owner of the business, not the poor ole guy out doing all the work. Well, it is true that God blessed me with the business. By the way, I believe it is God's business and I am just the caretaker.

I was raised by two hard-working parents who came from relatively poor families. My mom went to school for years at night and in the summer to earn her masters degree in education. My dad worked his way from a shovel pusher at the local refinery to a supervisor over the course of 25 years. He then started a machine shop and worked sixty to seventy hours a week. The man is now eighty years old and still comes in every day to help us in any way he can. I know what hard work is. I spend more hours at our business than anyone else. Over the years I have welded, done concrete work, driven a semi, and run a crane. I can't stand to be stuck in the office. I want to be where the action is. I want to be with my guys. Many are the times I will grab a welding hood and tell a guy to take a break. Romans 12:16 says to be willing to do menial work. I do not consider myself too good to do anything that any of my employees do. I hurt with these guys and their families. I want them to have another chance at getting it right. I want them to follow God and leave the worldly things behind.

I consider myself to be one of them, a working man. I take pride in my families' work ethic and I pray my kids will have it, too. We all want our children to have it better than us, but at what cost? I am afraid they will chase after the wrong things. I don't know if I want my kids working in these nasty old plants all their lives. But if they go off to college and live in a big city and make $ 250,000 a year as a lawyer, doctor or computer geek, what will they get out of it? They will want a $ 50,000 car and a half-million dollar house. They will send their kids to a private school where all the other kid's parents are chasing their tails trying to out-do each other. How will they find God in the midst of all that materialism? All I know is I better try to get it right while I have a chance and my kids are still at home. I need to get myself right with God first and then my family will have a good chance of following God. Then, no matter what they choose to do in life, I pray they will always follow and obey God.

This is what I want to teach the working man. I believe they are the easiest ones to bring to God with potentially the greatest impact for the Kingdom of God.

Why do I believe they are the easiest to get to commit to God? In most cases, they have tried everything else: drugs, alcohol, women, gambling, and stealing. You name it, they have tried it. What are they seeking? Are they trying to destroy themselves? Not at all! They are seeking what every person everywhere wants: happiness. Most of these guys have come from tough backgrounds. Their parents did not have much money or education. Many of them never went to church. Those that did never understood what it meant to commit their lives to God. And let's face it, wealthier people are just fooling themselves. They are covering up their unhappiness with the things of this world. If they get depressed they go buy a new plasma screen or take a trip to Vegas and suddenly they are happy again. I have gone down that road. No telling how many times I have convinced myself that I needed a new pickup for work, when the business was struggling and barely getting by, just because I was looking for something to be happy about. Luke 18: 24-25 says it is easier for a camel to go through the eye of a needle than for a rich person to go to heaven. I believe that. People put their faith in things, rather than in God.

So I can say that the working man is trying to find happiness and satisfaction in life. He has just been looking in the wrong places. By the time some of these guys get to me, they are really beaten down. As I have said, they are desperately looking for help, but they do not know where else to turn.

You need to understand one thing about the working man, they are independent. Some might say stubborn and hard-headed. They believe they can fix anything. They can build skyscrapers for gosh sakes. Why can't they take care of their little marriage problem at home? They can move a mountain with a huge D-9 Cat while building a highway sitting on the edge of a 500 foot high cliff, so why can't they stop drinking a 5th of Jack Daniels every night if they made up their minds to? They can ride herd over a mile of coal train for thousands of miles, why can't they figure out how to pay their bills on time? These guys are used to making tough decisions and over-coming obstacles. So does it make sense that they would surrender all their problems over to God? It is a concept most have not even heard of, let alone considered trying.

I believe their independent nature might be their biggest obstacle to turning their lives over to God. I went to church all my life and I never knew what it meant to surrender everything to God until a couple of years ago. I still struggle with it. I believe I was saved at a young age, but I was mired in living for the world instead of for God. I married a godly woman and we started a family. She wanted me to step up and be the spiritual head of our family. Unfortunately I left that role for her to fill for many years. In order for the family to function properly, the man has to take the leading role as the spiritual head. But before he can do that, he must first get himself right with God.

CHAPTER THREE: MY TESTIMONY

As a business owner with a working man's mentality, I am extremely independent minded. I am conditioned to making a hundred decisions every day and usually on-the-spot. People come to me for answers. I thought I was pretty good at decision making until about five years ago.

Do you know how hard it is realizing that you are about to lose the business that your parents spent all their lives building? I was actually to the point of counting the days until I would have to close the doors. We were heavily in debt, business was virtually non-existent. Shops like ours were going out of business all over the country. I would get an auction notice from a bankruptcy almost every day, and I would wonder how long it would be before we would be one of them. I was borrowing money on my wife's car and my pickup just to try to pay the employees. At one point the bank called all my loans because we were late on the payments. Yes, I fell back on alcohol every night just so I could forget about my problems and to enable me to get to sleep. Even though I considered myself a Christian, I never had considered "turning it over to God". I considered myself to be a tough guy and I believed I could get through it, yet the situation continued in a downward spiral until I had no money left and had lost hope. I finally cried out to God, "If you are ready for me to do something else, then I am ready." You see, God will try to take us to a place where we finally reach out for him. Usually, that place is when we hit bottom. Bottom is different for everyone. Some have to go through drug rehab two or three times while sitting in prison for using or selling. Some have to lose their families, because they are away working most of the time, or they are never content with what God has given them. For me, God had to get me to a place where I stopped trusting in myself and started trusting in Him. I believe that is the essence of what God wants for us: to trust in Him and not ourselves.

After I cried out for God's help, literally within two or three weeks the doors flew open and we had an opportunity to start doing construction work. Before that time we were just a welding and machine operation with nine or ten employees. Now we average between sixty and seventy employees. I believe that God wanted me right where I was, because we are still in business five years later and our business is thriving. It is nothing I have done. I was working just as hard before, there was just not much business. But by trusting in God, he has richly blessed us. And I am not talking about just monetary blessings. There never seems to be enough money. I am talking about blessings that truly matter, like having a positive impact on people's lives.

Crying out for God's help was just the first step. Not much else changed in my spiritual life at first, except I suddenly felt a calling to be a disciple for God. Yet for all the years I had gone to church, I barely knew any of the Bible. I have found that it is really easy to make excuses for not doing God's work, such as: I don't know the Bible; I don't speak well enough; I get embarrassed talking about God; or the best excuse of them all, I am too big a sinner, therefore I am not qualified to tell people about God until I get my life straightened out. Friend, let me tell you from first hand experience, you will never be good enough in your own eyes to do God's work. I have used all the excuses myself for not obeying God and doing His work. Ephesians 2:8-9 says, " For it is by grace you have been saved, through faith – and this not from yourselves, it is the gift of God – not by works, so that no one can boast." We can never measure up to God's standards. He does not expect us to. He just wants us to tell other people about Him. It is really simple. We are supposed to try to get as many people into the Kingdom of God as we can while we are here on Earth.

You do not have to be able to quote scriptures from the Bible. You do not have to quit smoking or drinking. You do not have to quit cursing, nor do you have to go to church every Sunday. You do not have to sing in the choir or be an usher. As far as I can tell, the only requirement to enter heaven is that you believe Jesus Christ died on the cross for your sins. Mankind makes it too complicated. Mankind tries to set all these rules and boundaries and makes going to church about as fun as going to the dentist for a root canal. Churches have driven more people away from God than brought people to God. To the working man of America, "IT'S NOT THAT COMPLICATED."

I am probably breaking every rule in the book by what I am saying about what is required to be a Christian. John Wesley is probably turning over in his grave. Yet I have seen so many people who claimed they were Christians and yet were so condescending and judgmental that it made me not want to be one. I would think, if this is the kind of people who will be in heaven, I don't know if I want to go there and spend eternity with them. It is hard enough in this short life to get by without a bunch of self-righteous do-gooders trying to tell us how we need to live our lives. Listen guys, God wants us to have fun and enjoy ourselves while we are here on Earth. He just wants us to follow Him. Put Him first. Tell your buddies and your families about Him. I have an employee who was saved some time ago, but he had strayed from God. He told me, "Ben, I have gotten so far away from God that I don't think He will ever forgive me for the things I have done." I told him that he may have gotten away from God, but God had not gotten away from him. When Jesus died on the cross, all of our sins were forgiven. I told him that he just needed to forgive himself and start chasing after God again as when he first believed. This employee has since turned things around and started obeying God's will for his life again.

You can be saved and fall back into sin again. We all do that to some degree. The difference for me came when I actually decided to trust God instead of myself. To get to the point of really trusting God with things big and small takes time. It is a process, not a one-time event. Sometimes we think that God is too busy to worry Him with our little problems. He is not too busy. He wants it all. He really is in control of everything. When I try to fix some problem on my own, I almost always make the problem worse. When I trust God, the situation always turns out the way He wants it to. It may not be the way I wanted it to turn out, but I can usually look back and understand what God wanted to accomplish. Sometimes He lets things happen to us to build our faith.

Our company is about to finish a huge job that we have worked on for eight months. There have been many times when I knew God was strengthening my faith by the trials I was going through. I have found that when things are going well in our lives, we get complacent and think we don't need God or we simply forget God. He has to let us experience trials and pains before we get to the point of turning everything over to Him. And He will never stop chasing us. He will always seek to win us over in whatever way it takes for us to turn to Him. Usually, that means some sort of obstacle or trial in our life. Most of the working men I know try to deal with these trials by trusting in themselves, by trying to fix the problems on their own. When the pain gets too great or the problem too big, they turn to drugs, alcohol, or sex as an escape from the pain.

This is perhaps one of the biggest reasons that I believe the working man of America is such a bright hope for a vast outreaching of God. These men want help, they just do not know where to turn. If a few of them will just try God, if they will turn to God with their problems, if they will seek to obey God's will for their lives, then can you imagine the possibilities? Their lives will instantly change. They will not want to live in sin any longer. They will trust God to deliver them of their self-destructive habits. They will crave being around other believers. They will find churches that worship God and share their faith with those in the community. They will lead their families to God, and marriages will be healed, and children's broken lives mended. They will want to read and understand God's word. They will be a disciple for God's Kingdom by sharing their love of Jesus with their fellow workers and give them something most have long ago lost: HOPE.

If you have taken the time to read this book my friend, then my guess is you are desperate for hope. You do not believe there is a chance for true happiness in life. You do not understand the meaning of life or your place in it. If there is a God, why would He put you here to be so miserable? The rare times of happiness you experience are engulfed by the pain and misery that life deals you on a daily basis. Sometimes the only relief you get is on your job. There you can stay busy and forget some of your problems. At work you can be around other hard-working guys like you who understand all too well the problems you are going through. There you can feel important, that you are accomplishing something. How many guys at Microsoft can jam 18 gears with a 550 Cat screaming while grossing 100,000 pounds while going up and down the Rockies with their jakes singing to you? Work gets you through it, but work does not bring you true happiness or satisfaction.

You no not have to know one scripture in the Bible to be a disciple for God. If you start living for

Jesus and your life is dramatically changed, people will notice. Tell the guys at work what has happened to you. That is all you have to do to be a disciple. Tell others.

CHAPTER 4: THE PHONE

I want to finish my testimony about how God got me to where I am today. As I said earlier, I really felt like a spiritual infant. I was forty-two years old and had gone to church all my life and I really did not know much about the Bible. Our pastor at the time was an older gentleman and I had grown close to him. He was near retirement and he had asked me to go on a spiritual retreat called the "Walk to Emmaus". I agreed to go and I sent my application in. When the time came to go, I decided at the last minute that it was more important to take my boys on a fishing trip instead, so I did not go on the "Walk". The "Walk to Emmaus" is usually scheduled every four months. For the next two years I would get a notification from the registrar of the "Walk" telling me I was signed up to attend the next "Walk". Every time I would find an excuse not to go. Of course by this time Pastor Terry had retired and moved away. Yet I kept remembering the promise I had made to him. And although the business had been saved by God's mercies, I was not getting any closer to God. I kept falling back in "the hole", as I like to call it. I would go to church on Sunday and tell myself I was going to commit myself to God, but by the time we got out of the church parking lot I was yelling at the kids. I knew something had to change, but I did not know how. Maybe I should call this book "A Dummies Guide to Finding God", because I really did not understand what it meant to trust and obey God.

In the winter of 2005 I received another letter inviting me to attend the next "Walk" in February. I finally decided that I would get it over with and go. Business was a little slow and I wanted to fulfill my long ago promise to Pastor Terry. I believe the Holy Spirit was working on me and telling me that I would find some of what I was looking for if I went on the "Walk". Since Pastor Terry had moved, I asked a good friend of mine who had been on a "Walk" to sponsor me. One requirement to attend a "Walk to

Emmaus" is that you must be sponsored by someone who had been on one. My friend said he would be glad to sponsor me. As the date approached, I started to get cold feet again. I was not looking forward to spending three days away from home with forty or fifty men that I did not know. Then a couple of days before leaving my sponsor told me that I could not take a watch or phone with me. They did not want us to have any distractions in our walk with God. I told him I could get by without the watch, but there was no way I was going to leave me phone behind. That phone is my life blood. As much as I hate the thing, that is how I run my business if I am not around. The business can not function, or so I thought, if they can not get in touch with me. Daryl, my sponsor, told me that they had the rules for a good reason, and to just suck it up and not take the phone. Of course my stubborn, prideful self did not want to be told what to do. So the night before we left, I plugged it in to the charger. And incidentally, the phone was brand new. The next day when Daryl came to get me, I had my phone neatly packed away and turned off so as not to lose any charge. When we got to the location of the "Walk" (You actually do not walk anywhere except from the kitchen to the chapel and sleeping quarters.

It is a spiritual walk to find God and it lasts three days.) I found an empty locker and put my phone inside an extra pair of shoes inside the locker.

All the sponsors left, and we did a couple of activities before we went to bed. The next morning during one of the breaks, I snuck back to the sleeping quarters to see if I had any messages on my phone. I got the phone out of my shoe and pushed the power button. A light flickered and went out. I held the button again for a few more seconds, and again the phone tried to power up, but it failed and turned black. I tried several more times using various combinations of buttons and holding time on the buttons and each time the same result, the phone would not stay on. I could not believe it, a brand new phone and it was already broken. Angered, I stuck it back in the shoe, closed the locker and forgot about it the rest of the weekend.

They were right! You get so filled with the Holy Spirit that you lose track of time. You do not want to be distracted by worldly things. Anyway, when I got home on Sunday night I was telling my wife and kids the phone story and laughing about it. Then all of a sudden a thought struck me. I wonder........... I went over to my bag, pulled the phone out of the shoe, and just barely touched the power button. You know what happened. The phone lit up and was still fully charged. I felt a rush go through me as if God was telling me, "Ben, I am in control, even of this phone". It was way cool. I still get a thrill out of telling that story.

Yet the real power of going on that spiritual retreat was in how the Holy Spirit moved in me. I was convinced that God had been preparing me all of my life for His Kingdom's work. At that point I still did not know what God wanted me to do, but I knew I was supposed to go out and be a disciple for Him. What a glorious feeling. To know that the God of the universe and Creator of all things actually was counting on me to do His work! And yes, He wants that for you, too. He does have a plan and purpose for you. You just have to seek Him out and be patient. You see, that is one thing I do not have much of, patience. I want results now, and I believe most of the working men of America are the same as I am. Time is money. We live with deadlines. Our jobs depend on results. If we are building or fixing something, we get instant feedback. It does not work that way in God's world. God's time is eternity. You may never get to see the results of your work if you are living for God. His purpose is to get as many souls into the Kingdom as possible. We are His soldiers. When God came to earth as Jesus, who did He seek as helpers? Did He seek out the philosopher, the doctor, the lawyer, the scholarly? No, He sought out the working man. Fishermen and craftsmen. People who provide food. People who build things. Are you starting to get this? You think your life has no meaning. Tell that to God, the One who made you and then avoid standing under a tree. He loves you and He is patiently waiting for you. Sometimes I believe we are such fools that we would not know happiness if it slapped us in the face.

I know! You are a tough construction worker. A hard-ass truck driver. You have fished for Ophelia crabs in the Bering Strait. You have welded on underwater oil platforms with sharks all around. You have taken on the toughest drug dealers on the mean streets of L.A. and locked up countless pimps, pushers, and car thieves. You are too darn tough to be a Christian. Christians are wimps. They drive around in their little mini-vans with cute little fish stickers on the back. They never break the speed limit. Hell, my Pete doesn't get warmed up until I hit 75. Sound familiar? It does to me. I was just like you. I own a construction company and welding business. If I don't drop an F-bomb on every other word nobody respects me. If I don't out-drink, out-Copenhagen, out-do everyone in the bad-ass department, nobody will respect me. I have to project a tough guy image, and Christians are not tough guys. I really used to think that way, and I will bet most of you working guys think that way, too.

CHAPTER 5: TEX

So now back to my story. When I got back from the "Walk", I was fired up and ready to do God's work, but I did not know what that work was. The church we had been attending had been on the decline for years, so naturally I thought God would put me to work there. But doors did not open for me there, and after a few months I began to get frustrated. Remember me talking about patience?

I was left wondering what God wanted me to do for His Kingdom. In the mean time, I was still struggling with what it meant to put all my faith in God. I kept having thoughts about having a Bible study for my employees, but all the pride factors would kick in about what people would think and there goes my tough guy image. And of course, there were all the excuses about not knowing the Bible very well and not being qualified to teach anyone about God. And of course the devil's favorite, I am not good enough. Even though the Holy Spirit was telling me to do a Bible study for the employees, I was refusing. I would casually talk to some of the employees about God, but I would never really engage them and tell them how Jesus Christ had changed my life.

Then one day God sent someone to me who would radically change my life and the life of my business. His name was Tex, and if you can think of someone who you know who is wild and has tried just about everything, Tex is that person times two. Tex was about my age with a wife and four kids. The oldest was already in prison. Tex was a good 'ole boy. Most of the time, he was a really hard worker. But life had dealt him plenty of miseries, most of them his own doing. He drank heavily, smoked heavily, and I am pretty sure he was on meth, because his teeth were bad and sometimes he would work like a madman while sweating profusely. He had been separated from his wife before, and his marriage with her was still very shaky. Yet Tex could do just about anything he set his mind on. He was not great at any one thing but pretty good at lots of things. He could plumb, weld, drive a truck, and fix about anything. Just the kind of guy you wanted in a construction business. He was also the kind of guy you really wanted to help. He wanted to be a better person, but he just could not get out of his own way. Every time he did one thing right, he would do two things wrong. I don't know if I kept him around because of all the things he could do, or because I wanted to help him get his life together. I hope it was to help him get his and his families' lives straightened out. It kills me to see hurting kids torn apart by failed marriages.

One day Tex came in my office with a wild look in his eyes. He said his wife had left him again, and judging by the way he was acting I thought he might go out and kill himself, or her. I told him, "Tex, the only way you are going to get you and your family straightened out is to get them in church". He said, "Yeah, yeah, I'll do it someday". He had his hand on my office door and was about to leave. Suddenly a voice spoke in my mind, "Ben, now is your chance, what are you waiting for?" I know it was the voice of God. So I said, "Tex, close the door and sit down". You see, in all the years I had owned the business I had never prayed with an employee, but I was about to give it a try. I do not remember the exact words I prayed, and it was a short prayer, but the power of the Holy Spirit filled us up. It was an amazing and incredible feeling! It felt like electricity running through us. At that point I was totally out of my comfort zone, since I had never tried to bring someone to God. So I decided to call a good friend of mine who is a pastor of another church and told him I needed some help with an employee. I told him I had prayed with Tex, but I did not know what to do next. Pastor Griffin told me it was his day off, so to bring Tex over to his house. I imagine Pastor Griffin had seen a hundred guys just like Tex, because he knew just what to say to him. He could see the hurt and pain in Tex. Well, within thirty minutes Tex was on his knees asking to be saved. Tex had finally gotten to the point in his life where there was no place else to turn but to God.

The lesson I learned was to step out on faith. Even though I had never prayed with an employee before, God took over when I became obedient to Him. And there is always help available. Do not use your lack of knowledge about the Bible or inexperience about the Christian life as a reason not to take action to share your faith. In order for your faith in God to be meaningful, certainly for your whole life to have meaning, you must share your faith. That is God's purpose for you and me, to expand the Kingdom of Heaven. Only when you get to the point where you can get past fear and excuses and tell the ones you know what God has done in your life will you experience true happiness and fulfillment. You do not have to go to Africa or Mexico or stand on a street corner yelling "Jesus Saves" to be a messenger for God. Just tell the people you know; the ones you are around everyday.

After I left Pastor Griffin's house that day with Tex, I finally began to understand what God was calling me to do. I had been searching for months for what God's will was for me, and all the time it was right in front of me. God was not calling me to be a missionary in a foreign country; He wanted me to minister to my own employees!

When I began to think about it, I realized that the people God had been sending me for the last several months had a lot of emotional baggage and were filled with pain in their lives. And now I understood why God had saved my business and what He was calling me to do. So I decided that it was time to stop making excuses and on the following Wednesday morning before work I would have my first employee Bible study. I thought it might just be

Tex and me attending, but I knew that I was doing what God wanted me to do. I had never led any kind of study before, so I really had no idea what to do. I went to a Christian bookstore and was looking at some possible study aids, and the one that stuck out to me was a book on adversity. Imagine that! With all the problems we face, with the trials my employees were going through, what a perfect book to begin our first series of studies.

When the first Wednesday rolled around, I was amazed to see seven or eight men show up, and Tex was one of them. We have been doing the study for almost two years now. I have some regulars and I have some new faces pop in once in awhile. I would like to have every single man show up, because I know they all need God, but I have learned some patience. I have tried to live by God's timing and not my own. I can see the Holy Spirit working in some of them, preparing their hearts. There have been some amazing stories. I sponsored twelve men to attend the "Walk to Emmaus" spiritual retreat. Several were saved and one of my welders, who I believe was an alcoholic, completely gave up drinking. Another quit chewing Copenhagen. Only by God's grace could they have done that.

As far as Tex goes, the story up to this point is not so good. For awhile he was fired up for God. He reunited with his wife and his entire family started attending church. He even got baptized and then he himself baptized his wife and kids. But when things started getting better in his life, he did what a lot of other Christians do, he started forgetting about God. He started going back to his worldly way of living. Drinking, and probably using drugs, judging by the way he was acting. We parted ways last year. It was sad to see him sink back into his old self. Yet I have seen it all too often. People get so desperate that they finally cry out for God's help. God changes their lives, things get better, they go to church for awhile, but they do not fully commit their lives to God. They never get to the point where they put their whole faith in Him. When things start going better in their lives, they lose interest in chasing God. It is easier for them to live in sin than to deny themselves sinful pleasures. They fall back into their old way of living and their church attendance fades away and their lives fall into despair again. Some will cry out for God again when the pain gets too severe. Others will decide it is easier to live in sin, or guilt will cause them to believe that they have fallen too far from

God's grace to ever be saved again. Yet Tex was saved, and God is always waiting for Tex to come back. God is the God of forgiveness. The great story about Tex is how by God sending Tex to me, I finally was able to realize God's immediate purpose for my life and the impact God has had on many employee's lives because of my obedience.

CHAPTER 6: STEP ONE – GETTING SAVED

So how do you do it? I may have painted a gloomy picture. Why go to the trouble to bring God into your life if you are going to fall anyway? I have long believed that getting someone saved and born again is the easy part. People get so desperate that they are willing to try anything for some relief of the pain and suffering in their lives. The hard part comes after being saved. No one said it was going to be easy living your life for God. On the contrary. The devil is real. He wants your soul to burn in hell. As soon as you start trying to live for Jesus the devil will unleash his attacks on you. But God is all-powerful and if you call on God for help, the devil must, and will, flee. The devil knows your every weakness and he will attack you when you let your guard down.

I am writing a book on how to bring our country back to God by bringing the working man of America back to God. So if I am a working man, and I consider myself to be one, then what would I want and expect out of a book, especially a guide book on how to change my life for the better? I would want the book to keep my attention. I would want it to relate to my circumstances. I would want it to be relatively short. I would want the book to tell me something I do not already know. And I would want someone to give me simple answers.

If you have gotten this far, I guess I have kept your attention. Now I want to give you a pretty simple list of things to do to forever change your life and assure your place in the Kingdom of God.

First, I want to explain the Trinity: The Father, Son, and Holy Ghost. I have mentioned God, Jesus, and Holy Spirit throughout this book. What is the difference between them? The best explanation I have heard is this, they are all the same. God is the Creator in heaven and his presence is everywhere. Jesus is God who came to Earth as man. The Holy Spirit is God's presence in us.

What separates Christians from every other faith? We believe in the only living God. We do not believe in the same God as everyone else. When God came to Earth as Jesus Christ He lived the only perfect life. He then died on the cross for your sins and mine! All of your sins were completely forgiven on that day. He then defeated Satan and death by arising from the dead three days later. Friends, if that one event were not true, then there would be no point in human life on this Earth. God came to Earth to die so that you can go to heaven.

Pray to Jesus now, right now, (you can say Father God, Dear Jesus, Lord Jesus, however you want to call God's name):

"Dear Jesus, I know I have sinned dear Lord, and right now I confess all my sins to You. I have tried living this life without You, and I have failed miserably. My life is in ruins and those I love are suffering because of my sins. You are my only hope dear Jesus. Please save me from myself and those who seek to destroy me. Please give meaning to my life by revealing Your will for my life one day at a time. I believe you are the one and only true and living God. I believe that you came to Earth and died for my sins so that I might be completely forgiven. I believe that there is nothing I can do to earn my place in heaven. Only by Your grace can I be saved. From this day forward I now know that my place in heaven is secured for eternity, so please help me live every day for You. In Jesus Holy Name. Amen."

O.K. dear friend, if you prayed this prayer and truly meant it, then your sins are now and forever forgiven. Praise God! A new soul destined for eternity in heaven! I look forward to the time, here on Earth or in a few short years in heaven, to get to know you and hear your story since you have gotten to hear my story.

CHAPTER 7: STEP TWO – FORGIVING YOURSELF

Now what do you do next? Do you understand that your sins really are forgiven? The ones you have already done and the ones yet to come? When God sees you he does not see your sin. By His grace you are now perfect in His sight. Does that give you the freedom to go on sinning? Absolutely not. Remember me telling you that you do not have to give up all your bad habits and quit cursing and things like that to enter heaven? Well, I believe that is true. But when you really get to know Jesus and He starts working in your life, you are not going to want to do those things anymore. You really can not have it both ways: living for God and living in the ways of the world. If you keep one foot in the worldly things and the other in God's world, you will most assuredly end up right back where you were when you started reading this book. God wants all of you, not just part of you. After saying all this, it seems that what keeps most people from moving forward in their walk with God is an inability to forgive themselves. When you prayed that prayer, God instantly forgave your sins, but did you forgive yourself? If you have been led to read this book then I am guessing you have done some pretty bad things in your life. You have a lot of regrets. You have hurt a lot of people. You have so much emotional baggage that it would take a fleet of u-hauls to carry it away. Step one was saying the prayer and asking to be saved from your sins. Step two is forgiving yourself, so now say this prayer, "Father God, I know you have forgiven me of my sins, yet I have left behind a trail of pain and destruction during my life. I know I have caused pain and suffering to those around me and to the people I love. I could not fix these problems before on my own, so now I ask that you would let the Holy Spirit guide me and give me the answers I need to heal the wounds of my past. Please lift the burden of guilt off of me and help me to live for the future and not wallow in my past mistakes and failures. I know you have a plan and purpose for me in this life. I want to turn every-thing over to you now. You are in complete control of everything. I want to put all my faith and hope in you Lord Jesus. I want to obey you and become like you one day at a time. Please take away the things in me that keep me from you. In Jesus Name. Amen."

You have now asked God to free you from your wretched past. Let it go. God has forgiven you, so you forgive yourself. Do not pick up that old baggage. Do not let yourself relive past mistakes. That is one of the devil's biggest tools. He will beat you over the head with it. When the devil comes at you tell him that he has no power over you, that you are covered with Christ's blood and that he must flee, and by God's power he will flee.

CHAPTER 8: STEP 3 – FINDING YOUR CHURCH HOME

So Step one is asking God to forgive you. Step two is forgiving yourself. Now that you are on the right path, how do you stay on the right path? How do you keep moving closer to God and not fall back into your old way of living?

I can tell you from past experience, you can not make it alone. You need support. You need to be around other believers who are spiritually stronger than you for support and encouragement. You need to find a church where the spirit of God is alive. Church alone means nothing. You go to worship God and be around other believers. You learn about the Bible and get instruction on how to be a better Christian.

And then we are to take what we learn outside the church to be disciples for God, fishers of men. Let God guide you in your search for a church home. Be very careful in your choice. A bad church can stunt if not ruin your chances of a meaningful walk with God. The church where my family now goes is non-denominational. None of the pastors have any formal theological training. The associate pastor used to be on drugs and was a bookie. His wife was the president of a local bank. He then found God and so did his wife. They both quit their jobs and went to work for the church. Our pastor was in the car business and then had a furniture store. He then felt called into the ministry. Our youth pastor used to be an electrician. At this church it is no big deal to wear a t-shirt or baseball cap to church. People are just glad to have you there. I am not saying that such a church would be the place for you and your family, but my employees who have attended this church enjoy it and feel welcome. There is absolutely nothing wrong with the denominational churches or pastors who have formal training. The important thing is you need to feel welcome and that God is working in the people of the church. In other words, it needs to be a spirit-filled place of worship. Is the Holy Spirit active? If not, keep trying other churches until you know for sure that the church and its people are spirit-filled.

CHAPTER 9: STEP 4 – GET INVOLVED IN A STUDY GROUP

B esides church, you need to get active in a weekly study group. Our church calls them life groups. There are usually many small groups that meet within the church. I am not talking about Sunday school classes. I am talking about groups that meet during the week on a day besides Sunday. It is especially important to be around other believers in a small group setting and discuss the challenges everyone is going through. As a general rule I believe it is best to be in a men only group. There are things you can discuss with other men that you can't with women present. Or you can do one group with men only and a different group with your wife in a couple's study. It is good to be around people with a stronger faith than you. You can discuss the Bible or get a study book to guide the discussion. There are lots of good books available. Those are things you will find out as you begin to associate with Godly people. My intent is to get you started on your walk and keep you headed in the right direction, not to bog you down with details.

Being in a study group is no substitute for going to church. They serve two different needs. The study group gives you the chance to bond with a smaller group of men who more than likely are facing the same things you are, or at some time in the past have experienced them. You will encounter Christian mentors, and as you grow in the faith, you yourself will be looked upon as a mentor to new believers. The walls you have built around your emotions will start to come down. You will begin to do things that you never thought possible, such as praying in front of a group. You will listen to other believers' testimonies and have the opportunity to share yours. You see, your testimony is one of the most powerful ways for you to witness to others. It is your story of where you have been, and how God found you and saved you. So do not put it off. The sooner you get involved in a study group the more likely you will keep moving forward in your walk with God.

CHAPTER 10: STEP 5 –
GOD'S WORD

For you to have a meaningful Christian faith, and a close relationship with God, you must read and study the Bible, God's inspired Word. It is His instruction book of life. There is nothing that you or I have gone through that men thousands of years ago did not go through. When Jesus was here on Earth, He lived through the same trials and temptations that we go through. He understands our sorrows and pain and He gives us a way to deal with every situation we face in His Holy Word. Each time you read something in the Bible God will reveal something new and exciting for your life. When you are reading God's word and you have a thought pop in your head and you wonder where it came from, or in my case I know I am not smart enough to have an idea like that, it is the Holy Spirit speaking to you and guiding you. When you are alone and quiet and reading your Bible is often when God communicates with us.

My suggestion is to take twenty or thirty minutes each day to read and meditate on God's Word. If you do it first thing in the morning you will start your day off right, but if you are like me, I am not a morning person and I have to get up really early, so I prefer to read my Bible before I go to bed. I then get relaxed and get a sense of comfort and I go right to sleep.

There are many versions of the Bible available in your local bookstore. I prefer the New International Version (NIV). It is written more as we speak today and is easier to understand than the old King James Version. Read and study God's Word. Make it a daily habit just like eating and watching ESPN. If you can make time for SportsCenter, then you can spare thirty minutes with Jesus. You might consider buying a study Bible. This type of Bible has cross references of other related scriptures in the Bible. The one I have has an explanation of key verses of what the Word is trying to tell us. Of course, God is going to reveal something different to each of us. Sometimes you can read the same passage a few days later and God will reveal a whole new message to you.

All of God's Word is relevant, but if you have never read the Bible before, I would suggest reading Matthew, Mark, Luke, and John. These are the first four books of the New Testament and are commonly called the Gospels. These books reveal the time Jesus spent on Earth, and you will marvel at His miracles and the love and compassion He had for all those He encountered. Jesus did not come to Earth to judge, but rather to serve others and sacrifice himself so that we could be saved from sin.

I would then read Acts and Romans. Find out about the apostle Paul, a mighty man of God. A true man's man. I can not wait to meet Paul in heaven. He was like you and me. He struggled with sin. He gives you an uplifting and encouraging message on how to continue in moving forward in your walk with God, and avoiding the pitfalls of living in the world. Continue your reading with Paul's letters to the churches in the books of Corinthians, Galatians, and Ephesians, as well as several other books Paul wrote in the New Testament.

The Old Testament is great and full of truths as well. I just want to give you somewhere to get started. As I said earlier, I went to church all my life, and I had a first graders understanding of the Bible until a couple of years ago. Once you start reading it, you will long to keep reading it. Consider getting a pocket sized version, too. I have a small NIV I carry with me and read when I am in the crane and waiting for the next lift. Crane operators spend a lot of time waiting. My little Bible has carbon black all over it. I like to scribble key verses down in the back to refer to later. To know God, you must read His Word. Psalms 119:105 says, "Your Word is a lamp to my feet and a light to my path."

CHAPTER 11: STEP 6 – AND MOST IMPORTANTLY, PRAY

The last ingredient to a happy and productive life with God is by far the most important: Prayer. 1st Thessalonians 5:17 says to pray continually. Does God really want us to pray twenty-four hours a day seven days a week? I believe He wants us to always have Him on our minds. I will admit, I struggle with this one. I try to get my day started by praying on the way to work, but as the day starts unfolding my mind gets drawn away from God. And then on the way home in the evening I will think, my gosh, I have not talked to God throughout this whole day. God craves our attention. He wants to communicate with us. How are we going to know His will for our lives if we do not stay in touch with Him? I liken praying to breathing. After a while, you do it instinctively. God is always in the back of your mind. You can praise and thank Him for your blessings and the many answered prayers. You can ask Him for guidance on some decision you are facing, big or small. You can ask for relief of some pain or loss you are going through.

For myself, I must constantly surrender everything to Him. I am a bit of a worrier, and God does not want us to worry. If we really trust Him, there is no need to worry. Easier said than done, I know. That is why I continually pray to surrender everything to Him: my wife, my kids, my business, everything. He wants it all.

You will begin to expand your prayers to include the needs of friends and loved ones, your church family, your community and nation. God wants us to do that. He can and will answer your prayers. In John 14:12-14 Jesus says, "I tell you the truth, anyone who has faith in me will do what I have been doing. He will do even greater things than these, because I am going to the Father. And I will do whatever you ask in my name, so that the Son may bring glory to the Father. You may ask me for anything in my name, and I will do it."

How awesome is that? Jesus says that we can do even greater miracles than He did. All we have to do is pray in His name and He will do it! God wants to give us a piece of His endless power. We get that power through prayer. I believe the reason more miracles are not done is that we really do not believe we can tap into God's power. Our faith is weak and we doubt God.

One important point I want to stress about praying is listening. If you are like me, I am the one doing all the talking when I pray, and then I wonder why I do not hear God's voice more often. We must be quiet and listen for God, in the form of the Holy Spirit, to talk to us. One good idea is when you have your quiet time, to spend as much time being silent as you do praying. If you spend fifteen minutes praying, meditate for fifteen minutes trying to keep your mind free of cluttered thoughts. Many times the Holy Spirit will put thoughts in your mind during this time. People often wonder, how do I know it is God talking to me and not my own thoughts. I believe a good analogy is this. If you put a hundred mothers in one room and a hundred babies in another room, and one of the babies started crying, that baby's mother would recognize her child's cry. Why? Because she has spent so much time with it. The same can be said for recognizing God's voice. The more time you spend reading His Word and praying to Him, then the easier it is to recognize His voice.

CHAPTER 12: SAVING AMERICA

Well, I promised you a short book. It is just a guide really. From one working man to another. Like my preacher says, " I love you, dude." I have an idea that if you are reading this book and have gotten this far, that you and I would hit it off just fine. We would tell some old war stories about our past mistakes. But I also have an idea that your life is about to change dramatically. Believe me, if you are anything like me you are going to stumble and bumble pretty often on the way to heaven's gates. But I know that once you commit your life to Jesus, you will never want to go back to where you were.

The average person does not see that God is active every minute of every day. It is hard to realize that we are a part of His plan. The working man especially goes through life grinding day after day. To some it is just a paycheck, but many get satisfaction out of the work they do. Yet almost all men do not believe that their actions have a significant impact on the world around them. Let me assure you brother, as a believer and member of Christ's army, your actions can have a serious impact on those around you.

As you start growing in your Christian faith, learn to be bold. Share your love for Jesus with the ones you know. My guess is, they are looking for the same answers and a way to happiness as you were before you picked up this book.

I would like to share one last story with you about one of my employees. About four years ago I hired an African-American welder. He has become a good friend of mine and I depend on him heavily. He used to sell and use drugs. He was an alcoholic and I am pretty sure he might have killed someone along the way. After his third or fourth stint in prison, someone gave him a Bible. He had tried everything else and had lost all hope, but as he sat in that jail cell the Holy Spirit came upon him and he gave his life to Jesus. He has not touched any alcohol or drugs since that day in prison nearly five years ago. God delivered him. He married a lady he met while in alcoholics anonymous and is helping her raise three young boys. She had lost those boys to state custody because of her drug addiction. Together they fought to get the boys back. He is now one of my best employees and is making a good living. He comes to my weekly Bible study. He plays pool at a local bar and talks to others about Jesus. God had a plan for his life. So never give up hope. That is exactly what the devil wants you to do. In John 14:6 Jesus says, "I am the way and the truth and the life." So do not let the devil deceive you. Jesus is the truth. He gives everlasting hope.

Do not be stubborn and prideful my hard-working friend. The future of this once great country depends on you and men like you. We can be a great nation again, but only if we put God back into our lives. I believe God is about to move in a huge way in our country. He already is in other parts of the world. And I believe it will be the working man of America who will lead the charge. Throughout our history it has always been the working man who was the backbone of our success, and the working man put God at the center of his life. Families were strong and marriages lasted a lifetime. And God blessed us. We have strayed from God and look at where our country has headed. It is now illegal to have the Ten Commandments in front of a courthouse. The non-believers are trying to take God out of the Pledge of Allegiance.

Let us stop feeling sorry for ourselves and fight back. Turn your life over to God today! Do not wait another day. Do not say I will do it later. God is there waiting for you. Turn your life over to God and go out and spread the good news.

After we find God, He calls us to be disciples and bring others into the Kingdom. You are the working man of America. You are used to doing the near impossible every day. So with God behind you, I know that anything is possible.

God bless you, Brother. I pray you will live a happy and prosperous life for Jesus.

SUMMARY

SIX STEPS FOR A NEW LIFE WITH GOD

1. GETTING SAVED
2. FORGIVING YOURSELF
3. FIND A CHURCH HOME
4. GET INVOLVED IN A STUDY GROUP
5. READ GOD'S WORD DAILY
6. PRAY CONTINUOUSLY

SOME OF MY FAVORITE VERSES

MATTHEW 6: 25-34

MATTHEW 7: 15-23

LUKE 8: 5-15

JOHN 1: 1-18

ROMANS 12: 1

ROMANS 13: 11-14

2ND CORINTHIANS 12: 9

EPHESIANS 2: 8

ROMANS 2: 5-11   EPHESIANS 6: 10-20

ROMANS 6: 23   1ST THESSALONIANS 5: 16-18

ROMANS 8: 28-39   JAMES 1: 2-3

ROMANS 10: 9

ABOUT THE AUTHOR

B en Conner was born and raised in Borger, Texas. He grew up working in the family business and after high school went to Southern Methodist University where he graduated with a business degree in finance. While there he met the love of his life, Anabeth (Annie), and they were married in 1984. After returning to Borger, Ben worked with his father for a couple of years in their machine and welding business. Business conditions became very difficult in the Texas oil and gas industry, so Ben began manufacturing concrete livestock water troughs for the cattle feedyard industry. He operated Southwest Concrete Waterers for 10 years. Also during that time, Ben manufactured custom shipping containers for the Department of Energy under the name Southwest Container Manufacturing. During those years, Ben did extensive welding, concrete work, and carpentry work. Ben assumed ownership of his father's business in 1994, Conner Machine & Welding, and renamed it Conner Industries. He sold the water trough business in 1996.

In 2002 Conner Industries began doing industrial construction in addition to their custom metal fabrication work. Ben is a certified crane operator and operates the company's hydraulic cranes. He has had a commercial driver's license (CDL) since 1991 and operates his own heavy haul semi-trucks and trailers to transport the company's construction equipment. During the past year Conner Industries has done construction work in five different carbon black plants, a fertilizer plant, and numerous gas processing plants. They are certified by the ASME to build pressure vessels.

Ben is an active volunteer in the Borger area. He was instrumental in the establishment of the Hutchinson County Crisis Center, a shelter for battered women. He received the "Daily Points of Light" award from the first President Bush and President Clinton for his volunteer work at the Crisis Center. He was president of that board for two years.

He was president of the Borger Rotary Club, and a past president of Borger Little League Baseball for three years. Ben has coached youth sports for many years in Borger. He also served on the Borger City Council for three years.

Ben and Anabeth have a beautiful daughter and five rowdy sons. Both of his parents still reside in Borger.

Ben is active in church and enjoys the fellowship of his employees during their weekly Bible study.

Printed in the United States
202662BV00004B/1-231/P

9 781606 470152